THE HORMONE WAY TO HEALTH AND HAPPINESS

THE HORMONE WAY TO HEALTH AND HAPPINESS

by

Ben R. Keller, Jr., M.D.

ISBN: 1-58820-616-5

1stBooks - rev. 4/19/2001

PREFACE

I have been working with women as their Obstetrician-Gynecologist since 1965. I am a "board certified obstetrician-gynecologist," and have been since 1967. I stopped practicing OB in 1987 and have done Gynecologic surgery and primary care of women since then. A major part of these recent years was spent designing Hormone Replacement Therapy (HRT) programs for my patients. I also did the latter for the first twenty-two years of my practice, and I did not attempt to collect data. The figures I use from my practice these past years are close approximations and estimates. I have always been a solo practitioner, preferring the one-on-one relationship with my patients. My approach to hormone therapy for the menopausal and post-menopausal woman is the result of learning from my patients and consequently modifying what I was taught on this subject.

We Gynecologists glibly call it "the menopause," but our patients refer to it as "THE CHANGE OF LIFE!" That is "pregnant" with meaning! We men do not contemplate reaching a certain age and changing into someone else. Women do! That is, indeed, a heavy concept. Long ago I decided that I would try to help my patients simply remain themselves and not have to become someone else.

I build a program for each patient that is custom fitted to that woman. I teach her that once we have the right program for her, she should feel just like the person she has been up to the time she felt her body start to change, not like Superwoman or any other person. That program is not set in concrete for the rest of her life, but will have to be modified as her body evolves and changes with the years.

The way most hormone therapy of the second half of a woman's life is currently done is to set up the program that a doctor likes and give that to all his patients. If that fits a patient, fine; but, if not, the doctor usually says, "that is what I advise my patients to use." And that is that! If a patient doesn't fit his program, she is out of luck.

Over the thirty-two years I have been privileged to practice the art of medicine, I have always taught my patients about their bodies and how to care for them. I have also LISTENED to my patients and learned a lot from them. I added what

I learned from them to what I learned from my formal teachers, from continuing medical education, journals, and a smattering of reason and logic, and I have developed a method for managing hormones that uses almost no expensive lab tests for hormone levels. Except for an occasional "serum FSH," (Follicle Stimulating Hormone - the pituitary hormone that tells the ovary how much estrogen to make) I use purely clinical grounds for evaluating the levels of hormones that each woman needs to remain the same woman she has been prior to "the Change of Life."

I teach my patients what I mean when I use certain words and phrases as we discuss their balance and adjust the program to fit them. One example of this is the terms, "hot flashes" and "hot flushes." Most doctors use the two phrases as though they were direct synonyms, which seems redundant to me. I use them as **degrees** of the same thing.

Phonetically, "flash" sounds more severe than "flush," which sounds softer and more muted. To me and my patients, "flash" means you <u>sweat</u> during the episode, and "flush" means that you stay dry and still suddenly feel distinctly hotter and uncomfortable although the temperature of the environment has not changed at all.

These are definite episodes and should not be confused with being "hot natured," which means you are always hotter than the people around you.

Menopause is the loss of the functioning of the ovaries, either surgically or naturally. For thirty-odd years, the ovaries produce estrogens, progestins, and a tiny amount of androgens (male hormones, about one to two percent). The male testes do the reverse, making 98% androgens, e.g., testosterone, and 1-2% estrogens. We do not yet know what that tiny amount of estrogens does for us men (perhaps it keeps us from being "complete jackasses"), but for the woman we do know what that 2% of androgens does for her.

It does two things: (1) it plugs into receptor sites in the woman's brain, chemical "sockets" in the cells, that facilitate the release of neurotransmitter chemicals that help the woman be emotionally more "positive" or enthusiastic about her life - a player and not a "wall flower," and (2) it is the necessary starting place for her libido, desire for sex, and the ability to enjoy that wonderful gift of our Creator to all of us. I'll talk about this in more depth later in this book.

When I was in training many years ago, my teachers, all men, used to say, "When you give women hormones to relieve their hot flashes, they may say that they feel mentally sharper and clearer. When they do, it's all in their minds, since estrogens do not transmit impulses between the nerve cells." They were wrong!

We now know that there are receptor sites in the brain cells for estrogens, and when estrogens plug into those sites, it facilitates the release from the cells of neurotransmitter chemicals that <u>do</u> make her brain work better, sharper, and clearer. Estrogens affect her intellectual functioning very significantly. There is mounting evidence that estrogens may even postpone the onset and attenuate the severity of Alzheimer's Disease!

This book is about how I manage hormones for my patients. It is not the way I was taught to do it by my professors, etc. in the profession, but the way my patients have taught me works best for them. Some authorities in Gynecological Endocrinology may disagree with my methods, but my patients do not.

I believe the aim of a good program is to recreate as closely as possible in the patient's blood stream the same hormonal mixture that her ovaries used to create in the years that they functioned normally. I try to "mimic nature" as closely as I can, since I have never seen anyone "best" nature when she is doing her job normally.

If we succeed, the woman should feel the same way her healthy ovaries used to make her feel. She does not experience the "CHANGE OF LIFE." If you are interested in how I use my method, read on, and I hope you enjoy the book. I wrote it mostly for the ladies.

To be "politically correct" I try not to refer to The Creator as "God" or "Him," but simply use "The Creator." I don't want to be called "sexist" or some other popular epithet. I am old enough to say that I was raised with a lot of "politically incorrect" terms at a time when they were still acceptable, and no one even noticed your using them.

I certainly have no clue as to whether "The Creator" even has a gender. Probably not!

CONTENTS

Ben R. Keller, Jr., M.D.

A PHILOSOPHY OF HORMONE REPLACEMENT THERAPY (HRT)

In 1960, my professor of OB-GYN said, "At the menopause, women lose the hormones that their ovaries made in their reproductive years. Some get severe hot flashes, but most do not; and a little phenobarbital (a tranquilizer) for their nerves is all that is needed. The few that have the severe hot flashes may need some estrogens to control them." We were not supposed to give hormones unless we were treating severe hot flashes.

Since then, such an overwhelming mass of data has been collected on the changes at menopause and the consequences that follow, that only a few "spotlight-grabbers" that love to get their face on national TV and like to play the role of "Renegade" argue against being sure that as many women as possible are protected by having adequate hormone replacement starting at the first signs of menopause.

We've heard the argument that says, "If God had meant for women to have hormones after the menopause, He would have made women continue

1

making their own hormones and only stop making eggs." My personal philosophy, which is shared by almost all conscientious gynecologists and other physicians that care for and about women, is this: I believe the Creator made this universe and set it in motion long before our imaginations can comprehend, and it has been evolving just as He/She/It meant it to, <u>and</u> the Creator does **NOT** tamper with that original design every hundred years or so. We were put here in this life to learn all the truths of this universe and to show our love of our Creator by loving and caring for our fellow travelers while the universe unfolds as it was designed to do from the first.

As late as one hundred years ago, the average age of the woman at death was only a few years after her menopause. The creator has allowed us to learn how to extend that life span an additional 30-40 years! Must we sit idly by and let those years be miserable, unhealthy ones? Is that the way to care for our fellow travelers? I think not. We have gained the knowledge to make those latter years good and full of activity and joy, and we should.

We are no longer treating "hot flashes;" we are protecting the integrity of the woman's bones and the important flow of blood to the woman's heart, while also preserving the health of many other parts of her body. The authorities on the care of women today are no longer having long debates about whether we should give hormones to women at and beyond the menopause. They turn to those of us who are seeing women in our practices and say, "If you have women in your practice who are not getting hormones, why aren't you doing your job, doctor? Why aren't you educating those women and convincing them of the value of hormones in their lives and health?"

Since we first developed the ability to provide hormones to our patients, there have been those negative individuals who have closed minds to this and try to force their views on the rest of us. They do "retrospective research and data gathering" with which anyone can make a false argument for their personal beliefs. They hold their closed-minded position to their ears like a "Linus blanket" and suck their intellectual thumbs for security. A potentially bright mind that is closed to new concepts is the Hope diamond buried under fifty tons of steaming dung. If they want to keep their minds closed and waste their gift, let them, but do

3

not let them drag the rest of us into the abyss of their ignorance and prejudice.

What are some of the examples of this negativity? There have been those who first said we were going to prolong the woman's reproductive years into their 80's by giving them contraceptive hormone preparations, "birth control pills." Experience has proven them wrong.

A group of nay-sayers in New England and one in Sweden come out with a new "retrospective data collection" article about once every 10 years reporting that hormones <u>cause</u> breast cancer by starting with a group of women that have breast cancer and going backwards to point out how many of them have taken hormones. That is lousy and misleading research. If I start with a group of women that have breast cancer and go back to see how many of them ate bread, I could say the bread causes breast cancer!

Recently two female "doctors," one a breast surgeon and the other a woman hired by one of the large networks to comment on medical issues in their morning TV show, did an evening show in which they both repeatedly referred to hormones as "drugs," as they scared a million or so women off their hormone programs by forcing their anti-hormone beliefs onto their innocent viewers.

The word "drugs" has become a catch word that immediately brings to mind things like illegal narcotics and such, just like the media people have used the suffix, "-gate" to evoke and brand whatever thing they are reporting as the ultimate evil, illegal, and bad thing. That is a basic technique in propaganda.

Those two women who called themselves doctors subliminally lumped hormones with heroine, cocaine, speed, etc., by calling them "drugs!" If they were really well-informed doctors, they both would know that hormones are no more "drugs" than insulin, which is given to diabetics when they have lost their ability to make their own. Hormones are a part of our normal bodies and are not "drugs!" If those two women are really graduates of medical schools, they know that they were never taught that hormones are "drugs," and they must have been blatantly dishonest with American women that night.

No, we are no longer treating hot flashes, we are using them as important "blinking red lights" that warn caring physicians that it is time to start protecting that patient's heart, bones, urinary tract, vagina, skin, hair, nails, and brain from deterioration that occurs after the start of menopause. It is our duty to help her avoid "the change of life," and very simply remain herself for the last half of her life. We can now do that for her, and we should.

My personal philosophy has always been to try to follow and mimic nature whenever I can. To attempt to do something better than nature is total folly. Long ago when I first started to practice and give women hormones at and after the menopause, I reasoned that nature gave my patients hormones without causing cancer of the endometrium (womb lining) for about thirty years, and that is the safe way to give them to a woman who has her womb. Twenty years later scientific research established clear reasons that this is true.

In the years that followed, my patients taught me the fine art of hormone replacement as I listened to them and conversed with them as a friend and advocate for them. Any doctor who really listens to his/her patients can learn a lot, but you must spend some time with them and not herd them through your office like cattle through stalls, "Wham, Bam, Thank you, Ma'am!"

We have developed a sort of clinical inventory of questions that help us as we build, together, a program of hormones that is a custom fit for each woman. To do this over the years, I have had to leave the recommendations of the authorities behind and not have any rigid maximum or minimum dosages. We are not all 1966 six-cylinder Chevrolets, wired and equipped the same. We are all different makes and models, and that is why each program must be built to fit that woman.

I suppose that, if we took blood tests of hormone levels (at $60 to $100 each) at yearly intervals of every woman's life from puberty to the onset of menopause, we might be able to use these blood tests at menopause to recreate the same levels with our replacement therapy. This would be enormously expensive and probably not be completely effective in devising her program, since a woman's body evolves and matures with each year. That is why my patients and I have discovered this clinical technique of determining what amount of each hormone a woman needs.

<u>DOSAGE IS EVERYTHING!</u> She must have <u>exactly</u> enough and <u>not</u> too much. There are consequences if there is too much and consequences if there is too little. If she is getting

7

the same amount and type of hormones delivered into her blood stream that her ovaries did when they were functioning before the onset of ovarian decline, she will <u>feel</u> and her body will <u>act</u> as it did back then. It is really that simple.

Many times a patient of mine has begun on her HRT program, and a well meaning friend frightens her with, "Oh, my God! He's giving you estrogen? Deary, you are really going to get fat!" That is a common misconception. I believe it is based on women being given the "one-size-fits-all" HRT program.

The truth is this: What happens to a dog, cat, horse, cow, etc., if they are castrated? They get fat!--from a <u>lack</u> of hormones! What happens to a woman's appetite during the last three months of pregnancy, when her estrogen levels in her blood are 90-100 times the normal, non-pregnant levels?--she is voracious!

From these observations of nature, I conclude that having either too little or too much estrogen will make a woman's appetite increase. If she has precisely the same levels of estrogen in her blood that nature (her ovaries) gave her, she will have no new problems with her appetite and weight. In thirty years of experience, that is how it works. If a woman is on an HRT program and is getting fat, the program does not fit her properly. Adjust it.

What about giving androgens (male hormones) as part of an HRT program? Will it cause her to grow a beard, get a deep voice, have adolescent acne, or gain weight? I will go into this more thoroughly later in this book; but, it will do none of these things IF she has only the same amount of androgens in her blood that her ovaries used to put there - no more and no less! Does every woman need androgens in her HRT program? Not in my experience. Nature provides this for about 60% of women at menopause, probably from adrenal gland hormones that the body metabolizes into androgens. The ovaries only made a small amount, and the woman usually only needs a small amount. The amount is determined by her response, and we have reached that dosage when her body and mind are acting just like they did before the onset of ovarian decline.

To summarize the philosophy, the recurring theme here is:

The HRT program must recreate the same hormonal milieu in the woman's blood that the healthy ovaries did prior to the onset of ovarian decline, and, when it does, she will feel and her

9

body and mind will act as they did when nature was doing it well. To arrive at that program for any patient, the doctor must ask the right questions and listen closely to the patient, making necessary adjustments in the program until the patient can say, "I am myself again!" One cannot allow any preconceived "maximums" or "minimums" of dosage to even be a consideration.

In a word, "Listen to your patient. It works."

THE OVARIES, DURING THE REPRODUCTIVE YEARS

This chapter is meant for the lay person, more than for the doctor, and this explanation does not attempt to be highly technical. Rather, it is an attempt to translate "medicalese" into plain English. As much as possible the "KISS" rule has been followed - "Keep It Simple, Stupid!" (That means me.)

The ovaries are located on either side of the uterus (womb) on the sidewalls of the pelvis. At puberty they start to secrete significant amounts of hormones, and soon after that they also make eggs. They do this in response to the secretion of "trophic hormones" by the pituitary gland, located under the brain. Follicle Stimulating Hormone (FSH) from the pituitary gland goes through the blood stream to the ovaries and tells the ovaries to produce estrogens. Halfway through the cycle the pituitary also makes Luteinizing Hormone (LH), which tells the ovaries to release an egg and, thereafter to produce progesterone. Estrogens tell the womb lining to "grow," making it thick and ready to accept the anticipated, fertilized egg. The egg explodes through the surface of the ovary and is carried in a sort of current into the Fallopian tube, where it is supposed to meet with enough healthy sperm to be fertilized in the outer third of the tube and start dividing into more and more cells as it is carried down the tube and into the womb.

The place on the ovary where the egg developed (and just left) changes into a temporary gland, called a corpus luteum, which fills up with cells and starts to secrete progesterone. Progesterone tells the womb lining to grow in a very specialized and very specific type of mucus-secreting lining, which will help the developing, fertilized egg (a ball of cells by this time) stick to the lining and start to burrow into it and implant.

Estrogens are not very dictatorial to the womb lining - they just say, "Grow." They do not elaborate further and leave the endometrium to its own choices as to <u>how</u> to grow.

Progesterone comes along in the second half of each cycle as a consequence of ovulation and says, "Yes, grow, **BUT** grow **only** like I say - become a glandular lining that secretes sticky mucus, and <u>do not</u> become any other type of growth." While a woman makes eggs, she does <u>not</u> get cancer of the lining of the womb. That kind of cancer only occurs when the woman does not make eggs and the wonderful, dictatorial Progesterone. Remember this fact as we will come back to it later under the section, "To have and have not...a uterus (womb)."

Ben R. Keller, Jr., M.D.

WHAT THE OVARIAN HORMONES DO FOR THE WOMAN

As we develop from a ball of cells into an embryo and hence into what we all recognize as a baby, we develop three sets of urogenital (urinary and reproductive) systems, the first giving way to the second, and the second giving way to the third, which is the one we keep. This explains why certain parts of the organs in that area are effected by hormones while others are not. Estrogens effect the growth and normal, healthy appearance and function of the ovaries, tubes, entire womb, vagina, lips of the vagina, **and** the urethra (the tube from the bladder to the outside) and trigone (a triangle in the floor of the bladder, formed by the entries of the ureters from the kidneys and the exit of the urethra). The trigone contains most of the nerves that tell the brain when the bladder is full and needs to be emptied. Remember this, as we will come back to it when we talk about the loss of the ovarian hormones.

Ovarian hormones also stimulate the development of the breasts, influence the

15

distribution of body hair and body fat that is characteristic of the female figure, and insert into hormone receptor sites in the female brain facilitating the release of neurotransmitter substances that make a woman's brain work better and keep a more positive attitude. Estrogens make her skin more moist and soft and less prone to wrinkle. They favor the deposition and retention of calcium in her bones and have a protective effect on the health of her coronary (heart) arteries. They promote the health and strength of her nails and hair.

Estrogens make the vaginal lining become strong, elastic, thick, and moist, which makes the intense friction of sexual intercourse well tolerated and even pleasurable.

Men start to acquire early plaques of cholesterol in their coronary arteries in their late teens! This process gradually continues as they age into their 40's and 50's, when they finally accumulate enough to start blocking some arteries and causing Angina Pectoris (heart pain) and Coronary Infarcts (heart attacks that kill pieces of the heart).

Women have virtually clean coronary arteries beyond puberty and through the reproductive years up to the onset of menopause, at 40 to 55 years of age. When the woman loses her estrogens at menopause, her coronary arteries start to rapidly fill up with those plaques, and, by 10 years after the onset of this change, the woman's coronary arteries look much like those of her male counterpart! This devastating change is largely prevented by good estrogen replacement therapy initiated at the onset of menopause, thus preventing the most common cause (44%) of deaths in the mature woman - heart attacks. No, breast cancer is <u>not</u> the most common cause of women's deaths; according to accurate data collected from death certificates, breast cancer (CA) only accounts for 4% of mature women's deaths.

The human body is an astounding collection of miracles, which prove, in my thinking, that it <u>had</u> to be created by a mind beyond our capacity to comprehend, and estrogens are part of many of those miracles in the female body, the most beautiful creation of all.

It is my opinion that narrow minds chase their philosophical/theological tails in a circle arguing the pros and cons of evolution and miss the main point that there <u>HAD</u> to be a Creator who made the human body. How HE/SHE/IT did it is a <u>minor</u> point, not worthy of the intolerance it has caused.

Whether the Creator's incredible intellect chose to make the body out of a lump of clay, a wisp of cloud, or guided its evolution from other forms of life, that Creator's "fingerprints" cover the human body inside and out! **<u>That</u>** is what is important to know. My career (40 years) of studying and working with the human body has firmly convinced me of that.

WHAT THE LOSS OF OVARIAN HORMONES COSTS A WOMAN

The answer to that question in one word is "**<u>PLENTY!</u>**" At the start of menopause, the ovaries stop making eggs every month and skip one or more months at a time, causing the menses to become very irregular. It is that egg and the progesterone that comes from the place in the ovary where the egg was formed that makes a menses come almost exactly 14 days later, if the egg is not fertilized. As the production of estrogens and progesterone falls at the end of each cycle, the <u>withdrawal</u> of those hormones from the womb lining makes the lining slough out - menses.

Withdrawing progesterone and estrogens causes a much more decisive and thorough slough than the withdrawal of estrogens alone. It is progesterone that causes the menses to have the uniform number of days of flow and amount of flow - the "normal period" each month. When egg production drops to 2-5 cycles a year, the menses become totally erratic in all parameters. Flow comes at irregular intervals, lasts a variable number of days, and varies in appearance from one day of "mud" to any number of days of bright flow.

The only aberration of menstrual flow that is <u>not</u> to be expected in the menopause is "flooding," soaking two standard peri-pads (Kotex pads) per hour for more than two hours. If flooding occurs, diagnostic work needs to be done to be certain that endometrial (womb lining) cancer is not starting. Flooding doesn't <u>always</u> mean there is cancer, but it still must be investigated and ruled out.

Women learn to put up with "bleeding" from their "bottoms" once a month for about 30 years; they learn when to expect it, to prepare for it, and to plan their activities around it. Women don't like having periods, any more than they like having pelvic exams (and I never had a patient that did like them). I believe they put up with periods because they figure it gives them the choice of whether or not to take one tiny wiggling cell into their body and make within their body a new human being - the most incredible miracle in which humans ever participate!

However, unplanned menstrual flow that may occur at any time, last any number of days, and be of no predictable type is "really the pits!" By <u>that</u>

time the woman's choice of having a baby is fraught with increased genetic risks of a deformed infant, and she has had her fill of making lunches, wiping runny noses, car-pooling, and all the other "joys of motherhood." She really does not want a baby this late in her life. This crazy flow has <u>no</u> redeeming value.

Next the production of ovarian hormones starts to decline, even though no one has told the pituitary gland, "the boss," that the ovaries are due to "retire." The pituitary gland starts making outrageous amounts of FSH, trying to make the ovaries make hormones as they used to do "in the good old days." The net effect of all this going up and down of the various hormones is "the hot flash!" These are really upsetting. Fellows, try to imagine what it would feel like to wake up one to four times a night feeling like someone just sprayed your upper body with a generous amount of warm water while you were asleep! In a word, "It sucks!"

Meanwhile, if you are one of the unlucky 40% of women, your sex drive "goes to H___ in a hand basket," you can't even have an orgasm by masturbation, much less during sex with your husband, and when you try to be "the good wife" and have intercourse "for him," you feel dry and irritated inside and it starts to hurt!

The loss of estrogens causes the lining of the vagina to go from thick, strong, pleasantly sensitive, very elastic, and moist to being parchment thin, dry, inelastic, and increasingly tender to any friction.

The urethra and trigone have lost their optimal health with the decline of estrogens, and intercourse rubs them vigorously as they are right against the roof of the vagina, and they may make you feel like you need to urinate during intercourse and after. You may even feel a sense of burning in the bladder during and after sex. Then the loss of health in the urethra and trigone usually make you feel like you need to void more frequently, including several times during each night of sleep, and may make you start to lose a little urine as you get the urge to go and try to run to the toilet - you start to wet your pants! (This is called "urge incontinence.") Now really, how much does a woman have to take?

The partition between the bladder and the vagina takes a beating and gets stretched and loosened by the baby's head resting on it through most of each pregnancy and especially at the time of vaginal birth; but the health of those tissues, thanks to estrogens, helps them hold up pretty well, maintaining enough support under the bladder to preserve enough of an angle where the urethra leaves the bladder.....until menopause administers the "coup de gras," "the straw that broke the camel's back," and takes away the estrogens. Then the support under the neck of the bladder and indeed the whole floor of the bladder drops that little bit further, and you start to lose urine every time you cough, sneeze, laugh at a good joke, lift, run, squat, or bear down in any way. This is called "stress incontinence." Isn't menopause a barrel of fun! But wait, there is more!

As the ovarian hormones decline, you lose the strength in your nails, and they break off much more easily. Your hair gets brittle and dry, and your skin requires more and more facial moisturizers in a losing battle to keep away the wrinkles and sagging of your skin.

Without sufficient estrogens plugging into those receptor sites in your brain and causing the release of those neurotransmitters, your "living computer" slows down. Memory gets less sharp. You feel mentally dull, and, for maybe the first time in your life, depressed off and on to some degree. Your enthusiasm gets dull and you start to become a "watcher" more than a "player."

That is what the loss of ovarian hormones does to you - at least, that is the part you can <u>feel</u>. What is the loss you are not aware of having? Read on.

Osteoporosis is the loss of calcium from the bones, especially of the wrists, vertebrae, and hips. Trabecular bone has this wonderful architecture with the marrow space containing millions of interlocking "bridges" called trabeculae, that give the bones strength and a small but vital bit of flexibility. Before menopause, when you trip on a wrinkle in the living room carpet, all you get is a rug burn on your knee. As calcium is progressively lost from many of these trabeculae they get thinner and thinner until they disappear, and the spaces between the remaining bridges get larger and larger. The bones start to look moth-eaten.

You are 65-years-old and have not taken HRT (because these devious or stupid female doctors on TV have scared you too much). You are active, vital, take care of your own home, gardening, shopping, and live a good life. You trip on that same carpet and your hip breaks and maybe your wrist, too. You are now over fifty, and, in this last half of life, the most **LETHAL** thing to do to the person over 50 is **make them be still!** You are immobilized by the broken hip, and multiple systems in the body start to slow down more and more. Aging goes into high gear. A year later you are in a nursing home, and two years after that **you're dead!** One study showed that a woman dies of the sequelae of osteoporosis every twenty minutes in the U.S.A.!

Or maybe your are fortunate and never have that fall. As the trabeculae are lost in your vertebrae, they got weaker and weaker, more and more porous, until the weight of your body causes some of them to collapse, implode, more in the front than the back.

If you are unlucky at that time you may get a "spinal stenosis," and the crunched vertebrae impinge on the spinal cord and the nerves as they come off the cord, causing constant and progressive pain in your back and radiating out from your back into the rest of your body. Every time you cough, a 5000-volt shot of electricity shoots down your leg! Are we having fun, yet?

If you are lucky, you don't get a "spinal stenosis," but only have milder back pain as more

Ben R. Keller, Jr., M.D.

vertebrae undergo compression fracture, and your spine bends you over giving you a lovely "widow's hump" and making you spend the last part of your life shuffling around looking like a question mark and staring at your feet all the time.

"Mother, hold your shoulders back. You look awful all bent over like that." Mother can't straighten her spine. It has broken and healed multiple times by osteoporosis, scarring her spine into a question mark!

But, how about doing as the "renegade" female, breast surgeon said on national TV, and wait until you see that you are really getting significant osteoporosis (by DEXA bone scan), and then start to take estrogens? While no one has done serial bone biopsies, rather radical and painful tests to sample the marrow of women, after they develop significant osteoporosis and annually after they finally start to take Hormone Replacement Therapy (HRT) to show that they can return their bones to their original architecture with HRT after that architecture has been lost, autopsy findings suggest that it won't work. I can't imagine having my bones bored into to get a biopsy (like "plugging a watermelon") to do such a study.

To the best of our knowledge, once you lose those dense interlocking bridges, you cannot build them back, but can only add calcium back to the remaining bridges that still exist, regaining only a small part of the strength and flexibility that the bones once had.

If you hope to have, in later life, the original architecture in the trabecular bones that you had at the onset of menopause, you had best never lose it in the first place. Start HRT as soon as the menopause starts, or, at least, at the **first** sign of any bone density loss on a good DEXA bone scan done every two years (Cost - about $150.00 each time).

These new scans only measure bone density and cannot see the architecture of the bones like a bone biopsy can. While you can improve the DEXA bone scan density after the bone has been damaged by osteoporosis, that does not prove that you have regained the original bone structure and strength.

Even if HRT caused a really significant increase in the risk of getting breast cancer, and I am not convinced that is does, statistics collected from death certificates (since these are mandatory, this data is above question) shows that in postmenopausal women 4% die of breast cancer, while 44% die of heart attacks, 5% of respiratory cancers, 5% of digestive cancers, 9% of other cancers, 4% of pneumonia and flu, 4% of chronic bronchopulmonary disease, 2% of reproductive tract cancers, and 23% die of "other causes," most of which are the sequelae of fractures from osteoporosis).

I have talked about preserving the quality of life and preventing death from heart disease, stroke, and sequelae of osteoporosis, but what about the quality of death if you die of breast cancer vs. the sequelae of heart attack, stroke, or osteoporosis? Several studies have shown that women who get breast cancer while taking HRT have much less aggressive cancers that are more amenable to treatment and cure and less severe in the toll they take on the quality of life at the end.

Few women stop to consider what the quality of life is like after a heart attack - constant visits to the cardiologist, repeated tests, cardiac catheterizations, coronary by-pass surgeries, multiple drugs, and having to watch your activity to avoid placing too much strain on the damaged heart.

Or how about living after a stroke for a number of years with partial paralysis, speech impairment, etc. Is that a good quality of life, or is that a slow, drawn out death that I would not want to experience. Personally, I fear that sort of death more than death from cancer!

Death from sequelae of osteoporosis-caused fractures is not a good, fast death either. Most women have significant pain in their legs and back after the fractures start to happen. As their bodies rapidly slow down as a result of the immobilization, the decline of health and active living leads to a number of years of living in a nursing home before merciful death comes to end that last part of life. I do not look forward to being assigned to a nursing home for a number of years before I "cross over to the other side." That is not my idea of a good "quality of death."

Certainly death is not just the end of life, but is the last phase of life for all of us. That last phase can be fairly good or pretty awful. As I grow older and move closer to that final part of my life, I make my health care decisions with a fierce eye to what sort of death I am taking the risk of having.

If a woman wants to bet her life with the best odds, she will tell her doctor when she has her first hot flash and start HRT! I'll discuss this more in the next chapter.

WHAT ARE THE DANGERS OF TAKING HRT?

Female hormones do stimulate growth and make healthier most of the tissues in the breasts and the female organs. All cancers are "bad siblings" of some type of normal cells. Lung cancer doesn't just occur in the lungs; it is **derived** from normal lung cells that have had their genetic codes damaged by something. We don't yet know for sure what did the damage and caused the change. It may be toxins, free radicals, viruses, or some things we have yet to discover.

There is mounting evidence that even those normal cells have inherited genes for that type of cancer, along with genes that inhibit the cancer-causing genes. I believe that something damages the inhibitor gene for that cancer, and the descendant of that damaged cell will be a cancer cell.

There have been papers published in medical journals about every ten years that usually do **"retrospective"** analysis and claim that hormones cause breast cancer. They start with a group of

31

women who already have breast cancer and go backwards to see how many of the women took hormones. Using that technique of data gathering I can also build the same type of claim that drinking tea, cooking over an electric fire, etc, causes breast cancer. And there are always the "headline lovers" that publish and get quoted by the media (who love to tell sensational, frightening stories) that say such rubbish as, "Our study shows that hormones double the risk of breast cancer!" What they do not tell you is that the risk increased from 1 in 500 to 2 in 500 or from 0.2% to 0.4%. It is the old "fear-sell" technique used for centuries by con artists, and it allows those "researchers" to force upon the public their particular bias and beliefs.

I have heard a statistic quoted that 5 of every 9 women will get breast cancer, and it is used to try to get women to do diligent self-breast exams and mammograms, both of which I strongly endorse. I believe that it is because a lot of women are doing these excellent cancer detection practices that many who get it are cured due to early detection, leaving a true death rate of only 4%.

Some time back scientists found certain, but not all, types of breast cancers to have "receptor sites" for estrogens, progesterones, both, or neither. They also found that only the types that had the receptor sites could be stimulated by the hormones. The other types of breast cancer don't even respond to the hormones as though they were a stimulant or "fertilizer."

At this time, I have seen **no** good, credible, well collected data that prove that hormones can **cause** breast cancer. To say that something stimulates or "fertilizes" a thing does **not** say that it planted the seed and **caused** it. That is a vast difference!

I explain it to my patients this way, "I can throw fertilizer all over a plot of ground year in and year out, and, if there are no seeds in that ground, nothing grows. If someone comes by my plot of ground and throws some seeds over my stockade fence onto it, and they take root and grow, then my fertilizer will stimulate that weed to grow bigger, faster, and spread wider. Once the weed is started by something else, I do not want to fertilize that weed, but the fertilizer did not plant or cause the weed! That is why I rigidly require that all my HRT patients must have at least an annual physical exam before I write the prescriptions for the next year's HRT. I must "open my stockade fence at regular intervals and look to see that no one has thrown seeds of some weed on the land, before I fertilize for the coming year."

Researchers are collecting data now to try to show that HRT will not be stimulating at all to breast cancers that <u>do not have receptor sites for the hormones</u>.

About fourteen years ago, The Center for Disease Control, a governmental agency, collected massive data from multiple health care centers comparing a very large group of women who had taken oral contraceptives (O.C.s, hormones) to an age-matched group of women the same size that had never had the O.C.s. The first group was designated, "Ever-Users," and the latter group was called "Never-Users."

To their surprise, the "Ever-Users" had 4-5 times **less** cancer of the womb and ovaries, and virtually the same number got breast cancer in both groups. This means that the hormones caused no difference in the incidence of breast cancer, while giving protection against cancers of the womb and ovaries! That was a huge study, done without bias or any chance of material gain. I trust it.

There are even some studies that conclude that women who get breast cancer while taking HRT have a higher cure rate and better survival chance than women who get breast cancer while <u>not</u> taking HRT. Similar studies have also concluded that women who get womb-lining (endometrial) cancer while taking HRT have a similar higher cure rate and survival chance than women who get it while <u>not</u> taking HRT.

What about endometrial cancer and HRT? There is a slight increase in the risk of getting this cancer while taking estrogen replacement therapy that does <u>not</u> include progestins. This should not surprise us. Earlier, I said that estrogens gave the lining of the womb only one command, "Grow." Progesterone was a very potent dictator and limited the womb lining to only one kind of growth, the normal, mucus secreting, glandular type of growth that prepared the lining to support the implantation of the embryo.

Now, if a woman takes estrogens <u>alone</u>, and continuously, the message to the endometrium (womb lining) is "grow," continuously and without any further instruction as to <u>how</u> to grow. Left with this dangerous latitude, it is no wonder that an occasional lining will grow off in the direction of becoming cancer!

I shall not attempt to quote actual ratios, as they differ with the study we might read. But, to illustrate my point, let's just put it this way. If the risk of getting endometrial cancer during and after the menopause is 1 in 3000, the risk of getting it while taking estrogens alone, continuously is about 1 in 2000. The risk of getting endometrial cancer while taking cyclic estrogens <u>with</u> progestins will compare as 1 in 4000, and the risk of taking estrogens <u>with</u> progestins continuously is about 1 in 5000. Progestins make HRT safer than taking no hormones at all.

The other risks of taking HRT are related to dosage being either too high or too low. If the dose is reached starting low and proceeding up in small increments slowly until the level is reached where absolutely <u>no</u> hot flashes or hot flushes are occurring, that is the level that the ovaries used to make in relationship to where the patient's body is today.

Authorities talk and write in terms of the minimum dose that will prevent osteoporosis or coronary artery disease which is for most women the potency associated with 0.625 of conjugated equine estrogens. That dose is usually not enough to get the woman to the level her ovaries used to make, and there are side effects caused by insufficient dosage, e.g., increased appetite and weight gain.

A rare patient needs to either stay off HRT or take a very low dose to avoid complications associated with other disease states, e.g., chronic liver disease, history of chronic phlebitis with embolism, breast cancer with positive receptors for estrogens and/or progestins, pregnancy, gall bladder disease, high blood pressure, benign muscle tumors of the womb ("fibroids" or leiomyomata), and diabetes.

If you have none of the above conditions, it is not a high risk decision to take enough estrogens to stop your hot flushes/flashes. Frankly, I have found that mild cases of high blood pressure in patients at the menopause actually get a lowering of their blood pressure with one kind of estrogen, estropipate, while other more commonly used preparations which have estradiol in them minimally aggravate the high blood pressure.

In conclusion, your doctor can stop your HRT if any of these things should develop, and the effects are usually going to reverse. In the meantime, you can avoid changing into someone else at the middle of your life and can remain simply, and delightfully, yourself!

Finally, we should factor in another consideration - **Altzheimer's disease**! In the last four years, more and more studies are proving that women taking HRT programs receive vast benefits for this disease. Comparing groups of women who have taken no hormones at and after the menopause, those who <u>do</u> take HRT have much <u>later</u> onset of mental deterioration (senility - outliving your brains), much less severe degrees of the condition, and a markedly clearer quality of mental functioning.

Does it make good common sense to let an unreasonable fear of a condition (breast cancer) that causes 4% of mature womens' deaths prevent the modern woman from taking measures to prevent coronary disease (44% of women's deaths), sequelae of fractures due to osteoporosis (22% of women's deaths), and prevent the horrible specter of physically outliving her brains and spending the last years of her life in a nursing home unable to even recognize her own family and those she once loved. I am only a mere man, but I would prefer death from breast cancer over death from Altzheimer's disease!!

The quality of life is very important, but death is not just the end of life. It is that last phase of life and should be lived to the best quality possible. To me, this means advance planning to influence as much as possible the choice of the disease with which we deal in that last phase of life and maintaining the right to keep control of our own lives through that phase. It is my firm opinion that all those factors are more favorably affected by good, individually custom-fitted HRT programs for the women of this time.

We have yet to see good reliable, unbiased, well done studies that truly, conclusively prove that HRT has a statistically significant risk of increasing the incidence of breast cancer. Even if a good study is done, I believe it will show only a very slight increase risk of causing breast cancer which will be easier to cure and have a low death rate. To avoid that possible tiny increase in risk, the woman has to severely damage her quality of life and markedly increase her risks of heart disease, osteoporosis (a woman dies in the U.S.A. every 20 minutes of osteoporosis) and Altzheimer's disease. **DO THE MATH**!!

Ben R. Keller, Jr., M.D.

HOW HRT PROGRAMS ARE DESIGNED FOR WOMEN

A. "To have or have not"--a uterus:

As you can probably predict by now, progestins are an almost absolute necessity if my patient hasn't had a hysterectomy, i.e., she still has her womb. To give the woman estrogens cyclically or continuously without progestins to channel the type of growth into a normal type instead of into endometrial cancer or hyperplasia (an overgrowth of the lining which can often lead eventually to heavy uterine bleeding) is clearly not wise, although there are rare situations when this might be acceptable.

Actually, there are some studies that raise real questions about the use of progestins negating to some degree the beneficial effects of estrogens on the total cholesterol, HDL cholesterol, and the LDL cholesterol. They are still trying to equate these effects on the cholesterols and blood lipids (fats, including triglycerides) with true effects on coronary artery disease and the incidence of heart attacks, but we are fairly sure that they are important.

The good news is that, even if they later prove that progestins do partially negate the beneficial effects of estrogens on the blood lipids and the accumulation of plaques in the coronary arteries, if the patient has had a hysterectomy, she does not need progestins. Finally, the ovaries make progesterone the last half of the cycle after ovulation and the ovaries make estrogens most of the cycle during the reproductive years. The premenopausal woman's coronary arteries are clean "as a baby's" until she hits menopause. Ten years later **without** HRT, they have almost caught up with the man's of the same age in the degree of coronary disease.

This makes me believe that once again, dose is everything, and, unless we give more than the ovaries gave her, we can afford some progesterone in a program without causing coronary disease. What is just enough progestin? - just enough to keep control of the sloughing of endometrium that happens in a HRT program.

While there are some nice advantages to having had a hysterectomy, I only do them infrequently. I believe that the patient should be fully informed of what her condition is and what non-surgical treatments are available, after which she has to ask me to perform a hysterectomy, if the symptoms of the condition are causing her enough loss of quality of life to make the surgery worth it to her.

No one, not an HMO, insurance review board, insurance entity's "medical director," or even her own doctor can accurately determine how much pain and discomfort another human being is having with any given condition. Only the patient can be the rightful judge of that!

With rare exception, no woman will choose to have a hysterectomy unless she is through having children and the symptoms are bothering her pretty badly, and no other human should have the power to deny her that relief if she chooses it.

On the other hand, I do not choose to examine a woman, find a condition, and make her decision for her to have the operation, as is commonly done. "Well, Mary, your bladder is falling down really badly. Your rectum is bulging up a lot, and your womb is falling down so low that I recommend that you have a hysterectomy later this month with repair work in the roof and floor of the vagina. I'll have my nurse schedule the surgery and let you know when it will be." End of office visit. I have never done that. Some call it a difference in surgical philosophy - conservative versus liberal. I have always been conservative.

We should not remove every uterus as soon as the patient has had her family, but no one should deny the woman that option **if** the womb is causing the woman enough symptoms to make the surgery worth it to the woman herself. Once she has completed her family, had a sterilization, or lived some years on contraceptives, the loss of the womb alone is a loss of the monthly menses. That's all! Few women lament the loss of monthly menses, and certainly not if she also has some really severe pain and/or other symptoms.

I, personally, wish we had the technology to force every man who says that hysterectomies are "unnecessary" unless they are for cancer, to have a monthly bloody flow from his bottom for which he must wear pads and or tampons in his rectum, until the age of 55! He should also have to live with low backache much of each month, loss of urine every time he coughs, sneezes, laughs, or lifts, and have to push on his bottom with his fingers each time he tries to have a well formed bowel movement! While we are at it, lets throw in some really impressive menstrual cramps for three or four days each month. Now <u>that</u> would be justice!

If you don't really need a hysterectomy to have a good quality of life, don't have one. But if you feel strongly enough that you do need it to be rid of the symptoms, ask your doctor for it and hope that he and your "managed care organization" (M.C.O.) will let you have it. Managing this situation with the conservative philosophy I use, I have never had a woman tell me later that she is sorry she had her hysterectomy.

Certainly, a hysterectomy done for some other indication makes HRT much easier and, since she won't need progestins, more beneficial to the coronary arteries of any woman. Take that to the bank!

B. Estrogens:

The woman's ovaries make three kinds: estradiol, estrone, and estriol. The only way to accurately gauge the potency of hormones is by using animals that are kept well and healthy and giving the hormones to them until a standard effect is elicited. This is then assigned a unit designation, e.g., rat unit (R.U.) or biological potency unit. This method does not harm the animals. The "mg" designation that is assigned to hormone preparations is standardized against these biological potency units. At the 1 mg. level, estradiol is supposed to have a biological potency of 12,000 R.U., estrone - 1000 R.U., and estriol - 150 R.U.

Years ago, the first pharmaceutical houses that produced hormone preparations, tested each "batch" of hormones against animals to discover the biological potency of that batch and produced the pills at a standard potency in tissue that would be the same at the 1 mg. level. Using weight (mg.) alone is misleading as to potency. 1.0 mg. of one batch may be up to three times as potent as 1.0 mg. of the next batch!

As new pharmaceutical houses have sprung up by producing "generics" at greatly reduced prices, since they have no research and development costs, lots of them are marketing "generic" hormones. They also do not bother with the costs of biological potency testing labs. All the estrogen preparations (brand name and generics) were tested for potency at the ".625" level by an excellent organization not long ago. They found the correct potency in each of the brand name preparations, but the potency of the generics varied from as low as .222 up to as high as .700! That will really foul up a doctor's efforts at fine balancing a woman's hormone program!

Naturally, all the M.C.O.s, insurance companies, and other entities to which patients pay premiums to get help with their drug expenses love the generics and put tremendous pressure on the patient to settle for generics, or they have their "formularies" that list only generics for which they will pay.

The pharmacists also love the generics, since they can sell them to the patients for less and still make a much bigger profit on the generics. The result is disaster for the patient's HRT program.

There is a choice of two lines for the doctor to sign at the bottom of each prescription: "dispense as written" (means generics are not to be used) or "product selection permitted" (generics are permissible). On all hormone Rxs I write, I sign the former and write on the latter (generic OK) in large red letters, "NO!" The pharmacist usually still tries to talk the patient into letting him/her dispense a generic! I wonder if their intellect is unable to comprehend the "N," the "O," or the "!."

Or perhaps it is that "hope springs eternal" in the greed of most of them.

Estradiol is the most common estrogen used in birth control pills, and most of it is derived from the wild Mexican yam. Yet, "worshippers of the great god, Natural," don't want to take birth control pills.

Estradiol usually mildly aggravates high blood pressure of a woman who already has that condition, but that can be managed, and she can still get the benefit of HRT. Estradiol does not push up the blood pressure of a woman who has a normal pressure.

Estrone or estropipate usually mildly lowers the blood pressure of a woman who has high blood pressure, but it does not lower the pressure of a woman with normal blood pressure.

Some M.C.O.s do not have estropipate on their formularies and require that the doctor fill out a long, tedious, and largely unnecessary form, designed to discourage the doctor from trying to help his patient, before they will approve and allow the woman to get the estropipate she needs when she has high blood pressure. Even after I fill out their obstructionist forms, they will not approve the estropipate. If the patient appeals, they just tell her, "No problem; just ask your doctor to fill out a special request form and you can have it." M.C.O.s use that sort of subterfuge a lot. When your first (and probably <u>only</u>) priority is the almighty dollar, that is the kind of health care you allow, and that is the deception that is used.

This is what results when you have people with only business degrees (M.B.A.s and B.B.A.s), whose only interest is keeping overhead at its lowest and profit margin at its highest, making medical decisions that require a knowledge of medicine and patients! As long as the public will tolerate this, it will continue. A patient rebellion is the only hope we have to hold onto some quality of health care in this country.

I have never seen a good study done to document it, but I have noticed less tendency to swell in patients who take estropipate than estradiol. That sometimes influences my choice of estrogen in a program.

The best estrogen to use in any given woman's program is the form that best fits that woman's body. That is what guides me always.

The most commonly used oral estrogen is conjugated equine estrogens (CEE), because that was the first one that was available forty-odd years ago. It is a good choice for many women, but not for every woman. There are several estrogens in it as it is extracted from the urine of pregnant mares. There is no danger of it being dirty or contaminated due to its source. I do believe that rarely a woman's body reacts to the horse chemicals in it by manufacturing something that partially nullifies its effects and causes us to have to use a higher dose than some of the other estrogen preparations. I do not know this to be absolutely true, but this is a theory I have, based on my years of clinical experience with many patients.

The oral preparations that I usually use are: Premarin, Estrace, Estratabs, Ogen, OrthoEst, Prempro (which is Premarin and Provera in each pill), and a few other minor ones.

Hormone preparations are also available in injectable form - hormone shots. These are usually estrogens, progestins, and testosterones suspended in some oil or in a form that will slow the absorption from the injection site into the blood stream making the effects last two to three weeks. Hormones suspended in water are useless in my experience as they produce only a short activity and a roller coaster blood level which is miserable for the patient. Preparations that I frequently use are: Depoestradiol, Delestrogen, Delalutin (Hydroxyprogesterone caproate - a progestin), and Depotestosterone (Testosterone Cypionate - an androgen.)

Estrogens are also available in "patches" that adhere to the patient's skin and deliver hormone into the blood stream gradually over three and 1/2 days to seven days. These devices require slightly lower doses usually as the hormone does not undergo "first pass" through the liver, as it does when the hormone comes from the bowel (when taken orally) through the liver before it goes out to the body. This makes a difference to some women's bodies and they respond better to it. In others, this seems to make no difference.

Some women can't use the patches because the adhesive is not tolerated well by their skin, or they won't stay on well enough. The patches are restricted in their usefulness by the fact that most only offer a few dosage levels and it is hard to find a dose that fits some women. Sometimes I have to use two patches on a patient to get a dose that fits that woman's body's requirements. Again, the dose must fit the patient. Some of the preparations that I have used are: Estraderm, Vivelle, Climara, Alora, and Fem Patch.

It is always best to try to find an oral and/or hormone patch program for each patient, if possible. Only when I have exhausted every effort to find a program that fits the patient well using the oral or patch method, I propose a program of hormone shots to reach the proper fit. For less than ten percent of my HRT patients, the shots work best; but for those patients, that is the <u>only</u> way to find a program that fits well.

Most "authorities" in the field of gynecology today assert that injectable hormones are not useful, as their absorption from the injection site is not predictable enough to give a good, steady blood level. All I can say to that is, my patients who are on the shots strongly disagree and like the injections far better than any other form of delivery. They feel best on the shots!

Unfortunately, since those "authorities" have felt it necessary to make their "proclamations," most third party payers have seized upon them as a way to deny payment on behalf of those patients who truly do and feel their best on the injections. I suppose that is what "authorities" are for, after all.

C. Progesterones (Progestins):

Progesterone is secreted by the corpus luteum (in the ovary) after ovulation, but until recently that was not stable once it hit the stomach acidity and could not be taken orally. By injection, it has a short life when dissolved in water and a little longer life if suspended in oil. Therefore, it had limited usefulness.

Recently they have come out with "micronized" progesterone, a process that protects it from destruction by the stomach's acid and makes it useful for oral administration. Results with this have been most promising and there seems to be less side effects than the most commonly used progestin, medroxyprogesterone acetate (MPA), "Provera."

Provera has the side effect of causing a significant percentage of women to have some depression on doses higher than 2.5 mg. daily. I've used Provera as part of oral HRT programs for many years. The other oral progestin I use is "Prometrium," the micronized progesterone.

Hydroxyprogesterone Caproate (Delalutin) is an acetate of progesterone, but it is only available and useful by injection. It is very useful in injectable HRT programs, when needed. An injection of it usually lasts about two weeks. I have also used it successfully in a number of cases of habitual abortion due to "Inadequate Corpus Luteum Syndrome," ladies who have had three consecutive first trimester miscarriages, and all six women had normal babies after the treatment. One woman had three normal babies after Delalutin treatment, and then had her tubes tied! I've also used it to stop premature labor in one case, where it was more effective than the most commonly used drug for putting the irritable uterus at rest. The dose in these cases was 250 mg. per week.

D. Androgens (Testosterones):

I have only used two oral androgens in my HRT programs, methyl testosterone (MT), and fluoxymesterone (Halotestin). Halotestin is about 7 times as potent as methyl testosterone, and it has a lower side effect profile even at its higher potency. One oral preparation is called Estratest and Estratest HS; the former has 1.25 mg. of estradiol with 2.5 mg. of methyltestosterone and the latter has half that dosage of each. The other oral preparation is called Halotestin, and it comes in 2, 5, and 10 mg. doses. I have not found it necessary to use the 10 mg. dosage.

The injectables I use with androgens in them are Depotestosterone (Testosterone Cypionate) and Depotestadiol (a combination of Estradiol Cypionate 2 mg plus Testosterone Cypionate 50 mg. per c.c.).

How I build an HRT program for a woman is to start out on a low dose of oral estrogen and gradually move the dose up to what will completely stop her hot flashes/flushes. I would stress that we are no longer treating the flashes/flushes, but are using them as a pretty reliable "blinking red light" that is the human body's way of saying, "I need estrogens!" There are no "sacred cows" in this dosage, no arbitrary limits to the dose as recommended by the "authorities."

The only woman I have had in my 33-year career who got deep venous thrombosis while on an HRT program was on conjugated equine estrogens at the .625 mg. level--one of the lowest levels and the level most commonly recommended by the "authorities!" None of my patients on higher dosages of estrogens have had any of the complications listed by the experts as reasons for not using more than .625 mg. of estrogens.

I believe the reason for this fact is that a woman's body tolerates well, without side effects, the estrogen levels that her ovaries make for their active life. When her ovaries made that dosage for her for thirty years, she had **no** hot flashes/flushes and no side effects or increased incidence of hormone-related complications. Therefore, it seems logical to me that if we seek that same dosage for her (to the cessation of flashes/flushes), it should do nothing harmful to her. I have no "double blinded, randomized, crossover studies" to support my theory, but my experience for 32 years of building HRT programs for women has encountered no significant incidence of HRT-related complications. In short, it works! The range of hormone levels made by the ovaries of women vary from woman to woman, and the HRT programs that fit women vary just as much.

After we have arrived at the dosage of estrogens (and progesterones if the womb is still a part of her body), I ask the question, "Is your libido (sex drive) just the same as it was when your ovaries were working normally?" If her answer is, "What sex drive?" I start to add minute amounts of androgens to her HRT program and move the dose up in small steps to the point that she can say, "I am myself again!" When we reach that point I feel that she now has the same hormone "soup" in her blood stream that her ovaries gave her for thirty years.

E. When to "cycle" and When to Do Continuous Hormones

If the woman has no womb, the program should always be "continuous." When the woman still has her womb we must decide whether to "cycle" and when to do "continuous."

The dosage of progesterone needed, if a woman has her womb, is found at the point that her periods, when she is on a cyclic program, are like they used to be and are well controlled. If she is on a continuous program, with estrogens and progesterones taken every day without pause, that dose is the one that does not allow any breakthrough bleeding. Bleeding when hormones are withdrawn from the system is called "withdrawal bleeding," and when it occurs while she is still taking the hormones, it's called "breakthrough bleeding." The former is acceptable; the latter is not.

If the patient is at the beginning of menopause, attempting to do continuous delivery is fraught with frequent, unpredictable breakthrough bleeding. Western women may tolerate a monthly period at an expected time, but bleeding as a surprise is just atrocious and will not be allowed! Therefore, it is usually better to cycle the hormones, in a fashion that nature has done it in past years, until the womb shows signs that it will cooperate with a "continuous" effort. We usually do "cyclic" until withdrawal flow becomes negligible for three or more cycles. (The cycles can be one to three months long, as we wish to try.) Then we can usually go to a cyclic mode with only one or two short bouts of breakthrough bleeding the first year and none after that.

If the woman is well into menopause and has had no bleeding for three or more years before we start HRT, we can usually get away with starting in the "continuous" mode.

A few women on cyclic programs complain of some degree of depression on the dose of progesterones that control their periods. We then try to find a progestin that works for them without this side effect. If that can't be found, I recommend that she stop the HRT program until she loses the uterus or her body changes and doesn't require that high a dosage to get menstrual control. We are trying to preserve the health of multiple parts of her body with HRT, but most of all we are trying to preserve the quality of life of each woman as best we can. Causing depression with any therapy is not giving them a good quality of life. Depression is awful!

Now, let's get to the "nuts and bolts" of HRT building. That is done with my "objective inventory," the method of "listening to the patient's body." After we complete that at each visit while we are arriving at the final program for that patient, we have an open discussion of all her observations of her responses to the program, positive and negative.

Once again, the wide variation in the human body's responses to anything is a constant revelation to me, as I have heard many unique and highly individual symptoms women have attributed to a change in dosage or composition of their programs. I do not ignore or discount any of these symptoms, and I regard them as expressions of each patient's individuality. Either adjustments are made to get rid of the symptom or the woman has to agree to tolerate that symptom, if she is to enjoy the rest of the benefits of HRT. It is her decision, and it should be. I always try my best to get rid of the symptom, as I believe deeply in the value of the benefits.

The "objective inventory" is as follows:

1. The average number of hot flashes per waking day/per sleeping night. A sign that estrogen dosage is very low.
2. The number of hot flushes per waking day/per sleeping night. A sign that estrogen dosage is slightly low.
3. Breast soreness that is more than her ovaries used to cause her in their normal life-yes or no. This is sometimes a sign that estrogen dosage is too high.
4. Water retention, swelling, that is new and different. This may also be a sign of dosage being too high.
5. Quality of sleep; are there any wake-ups for no apparent reason?

6. Libido? I do not ask this one until after 1. and 2. above are at zero.
7. Subjective discussion of her observations.

It is important that we specify that these questions are to be answered only after a three-week adjustment period has passed. I see my HRT patients every six weeks, allowing for the three weeks of adjustment to occur and three weeks of post-adjustment observations to be made. It is folly to draw conclusions from her body's behavior during the adjustment phase. During that time, she may have alternating symptoms of being too high with symptoms of being too low every three or four days. She may be at the exact correct dosage, but we will not know that until the adjustment phase is over. Therefore, the 4th, 5th, and 6th weeks are what we discuss on the inventory. The patient is encouraged to "hang in there" during the adjustment phase unless it is just unbearable, and to call me before stopping or changing the dosage herself. If the patient changes her dosage by herself during that adjustment phase, we do not have a clue as to where we really stand at the next review.

In the three weeks <u>after</u> the adjustment is over her body will produce a <u>consistent</u> picture that she is too low, too high, or right on the correct dose for her body. That is often at the first one or two return appointments after starting the HRT program. Less frequently, it takes three or more return appointments with an inventory each time to arrive at the level that fits the patient.

There are some qualifying remarks that must be made about some of the inventory questions:

"3." If the dose causes the same minimal breast tenderness that her ovaries used to cause, we are probably at the same level of estrogen that her ovaries made. If the breast tenderness is more than that, it may mean that the estrogen dose is too high, but not in all cases. Some women have some degree of "fibrocystic condition" of the breasts, which will make her breasts overreact to a normal level of estrogens, whether their ovaries are making her estrogens (prior to menopause) or we are giving her estrogens after the menopause has started and beyond.

Fibrocystic condition exists when fibrocytes, the cells that our bodies use to build scar tissue, migrate into the breasts setting up strands and sheets of scar tissue that make the breasts feel thickened and lumpy, especially in the upper-outer quadrants of the breasts. This also causes some women to have cysts (pockets of fluid) in their breasts; hence the term "fibro cystic."

We do not know what causes this condition to occur, but it can occur early in a few women's reproductive years and more and more commonly the older women get. It occurs in a majority of women from the mid-thirties on. It is usually slowly progressive, and elderly women commonly have significant soreness and tenderness due to this condition. It varies widely in severity from woman to woman at any age.

If I have a patient who has it to an advanced degree and it is causing pain and tenderness before menopause, I often use an androgen, e.g., testosterone or danazol, in small doses to curtail the fibrocystic breast's reaction to her own, normal estrogen.

If this condition is found on the physical exam of a menopausal HRT patient, we have arrived at the minimal dose necessary to stop the hot flashes/flushes in small increments, and the patient does not have any increased water retention (the other sign that estrogen dose may be too high), I conclude that her fibrocystic condition is causing her breasts to overreact to the level of estrogen that the rest of her body requires for optimal health. I, then, treat her exactly like I would a premenopausal woman with symptomatic fibrocystic condition and leave her estrogen level in her HRT program as it is.

If a patient does have fibrocystic breasts, I teach her to manipulate her dietary intake of Methylxanthines, leaving them off when her breasts become sore and tender, and allowing herself some of them when her breasts are comfortable. Methylxanthines are caffeine, theophylline, theobromine and a few minor ones found in coffee, tea (caffeine and theophylline), chocolate, and all brown colas, e.g., Coca-Cola, Pepsi, Dr Pepper, etc.

"4." Some patients have a tendency for a degree of water retention (swelling) most of their lives, especially severely overweight people. If these patients do not have an increase in their swelling while we reach their hot flush-stopping dose of estrogens, I regard this as not being a problem and not a sign of estrogen dosage being too high. In some cases, swelling is a sign of poorly functioning kidneys; but in most cases of mild to moderate swelling, we don't have a clue as to why they swell and it is termed "idiopathic edema." In these cases, all the standard tests of kidney function are normal, and the patient still retains a bit too much water all the time. If an HRT patient has <u>both</u> increased swelling and sore breasts on HRT, I strongly suspect that her dose of estrogens is too high.

I mentioned earlier that some forms of estrogen have more tendency to cause water retention at any dose than others. This fact influences our choice of type of hormone in some patients.

"5." Quality of sleep may be poor for a number of reasons. Many patients admit that they slept poorly, waking multiple times during each night's sleep before they became menopausal. I, then, modify this question to stress, "Are you waking <u>more</u> often than you used to since menopause started?"

Some patients have bladder dysfunction called "nocturia," which means they are awakened one or more times each night with a strong need to urinate. I won't go into the reasons for this here, but those times are not counted as "wake-ups" without a reason" for our inventory.

With this question we are seeking times when the patient wakes up, looks at her bedside clock, discovers it is not time to get up yet, and goes back to sleep. These are probably "occult hot flushes! No professor taught me this one. My menopausal patients taught me this! Early in my career, I started to encounter patients who would comment after we had reached their proper dose of estrogens, "Can these hormones make me sleep better?" When I was young and "all-knowing," I would scoff and say, "Of course, not. These are only hormones, <u>not</u> sedatives."

However, I kept hearing that statement over and over until I was forced to try to explain it in some logical way. I finally realized that these were hot flushes (dry) which were hitting the woman when she was at a deep plane of sleep, jarring her body and <u>starting</u> her mind on its way to the surface of consciousness, but the heat was gone by the time she became completely awake! Hot fl<u>a</u>shes are easy to identify at night, because the woman wakes with wet hair, and sometimes her gown and even her bed is wet from the sweating that occurs with a hot flash. A hot fl<u>u</u>sh does not cause any sweating. Thus, "wake-ups for no reason" mean that the dose of estrogen is not up to the level her ovaries used to make. Once again, my patients taught me an important lesson.

"6." Libido (sex drive): It has been my observation that about 6 out of 10 patients that are in and beyond the menopause have no loss of sex drive. I believe these lucky ladies are getting sufficient secretion of androgens from their adrenal glands, two little all-important glands that sit on top of the kidneys, to preserve their normal libido after the ovaries stop making the small bit of male hormone.

The other four women have a total loss of sexual desire or interest and can't have a normal orgasm no matter how well the clitoris is stimulated. If we put these four women on HRT programs with a level of estrogens that totally stops their hot flashes/flushes, they all can convert a tiny amount of the estrogens into testosterone or a similar androgen, but only one of them can convert enough into androgens to regain her original drive and response to sexual stimulation. The other three still will have no sex drive and can't even successfully masturbate. Only these three women will need androgens in her program. That is why I wait until we have stopped all the hot flashes/flushes before I even ask about their sex drive.

Am I a "sex fiend doctor" who wants all his patients to be sex crazed people? Not at all. What I am really after is restoring the normal amount of androgens to each patient so they can enjoy <u>both</u> functions of these androgens: 1. A positive mood and attitude, and 2. A normal libido (sex drive) and capacity for normal sexual sensitivity and response.

If there are normal amounts of androgens in her body, they insert into receptor sites <u>in the brain</u> cells, facilitating the release from those cells of other neurotransmitter chemicals that affect her mood and positiveness of attitude.

For lack of this, the woman who has never been depressed starts to have periods of depression as never before, and the woman who used to have some mild depressive episodes before menopause starts to have them more often, more severely, and they last longer. She loses her positive attitude, her zest for life, her aggressiveness at pursuing the active enjoyment of her life, her "joie d' vivre!" She becomes a "wall flower" and is no longer a "player."

Regaining this healthy attitude and positiveness is what I am **really** after when I ask about her libido, but I cannot easily and rapidly measure how positive she is. It is too difficult to measure, short of a 16-page questionnaire on attitude at each visit. I <u>can</u> measure her libido and very exactly. That is the second thing those androgens do for the woman, the "2."

I use the second thing, her libido, as a measuring device to ascertain when we have just enough androgens <u>and not too much</u>. The logic I use is this: If we can find the dosage of androgens that her ovaries gave her during their normal years, we will reproduce the <u>same</u> drive she had back then, no more and no less. If we are accurate in doing this we should not get any more of the masculinizing effects (male distribution hair growth, deepening of the voice, etc.) than her ovaries caused and that was none. If her ovaries could get away with giving her a given dose of androgens without causing unwanted side effects, we should be able to do the same, if the dose we use is the exact same. That works, and it works well.

If she used to be a "twice-a-month" girl, we want her to become again a "twice-a-month" girl. If she was a "twice-a-week" or "twice-a-day" girl before, we want her to become exactly that again, no more and no less. We ask her to look back at her twenties and thirties and try to remember as accurately as possible what frequency she would have liked to have sex then.

We stress that this is not asking what frequency she actually <u>had</u> sex then, for that is usually a compromise between <u>her</u> drive and her <u>partner's</u> drive. We ask her to remember what frequency she would have <u>preferred</u> to have if the issue was left entirely up to her alone. That becomes our goal in doing now what her ovaries did in this area then.

The patient no longer needs to tell me what her previous libido was. That is her private stuff. (Some patients **did** share that with me as I was formulating this means of measuring the response. They taught me how to do this.)

A widow taught me the other way to measure the second parameter. When we got to this phase of working on her total program, I asked her about her sex drive, and she responded, "How would I know. John has been dead for eight months!" I flushed and said, "I'm sorry. I did not mean to be insensitive. I use this to determine whether you need testosterone and how much you need to be in complete balance." She said, "Well, I'm **not** going out and get some man just so I can get my hormones just right!"

In fact, she had become a recluse since her husband's death following a long period of almost total invalidism. She only left her home to get groceries, and did not go out otherwise. This was part of the reason I believed she was depressed as well as grieving. I was truly worried about her. The grief was one thing, but I felt the depression was making it even worse.

I racked my brain for a moment, and then I asked," Do you masturbate?" She said listlessly, "No, I don't need it."

I then asked, "What happened the last time you tried?" She replied with some disgust, "That's the point. It's not worth the effort - an hour and a half later and nothing! Who needs that?"

I said, "I agree, but that answers my question. You do need some testosterone in order for that to work. We can use that for our measuring stick! Start taking this Halotestin 5 mg. tablet once a week for three weeks (Level I). Our goal will be to reach the point that your efforts yield the old results in the same length of time as before. If that was 15 minutes and you haven't been successful by 15 minutes, stop and don't pursue it further. Go to the next level with a tablet twice a week for three weeks, and try again the same way. When you get to the correct level, at the end of the three weeks, it will work as it used to."

She came back twelve weeks later, sat down quietly in her chair and said, "Well, it works again!" I responded, "That's wonderful! What level are you on?" She said, "Level III."

I said, "That is what we needed to know. I don't care whether you masturbate again or not. You should now get the other effect I wanted for you. Are you getting out of the house occasionally?"

She answered, "Well, I'm still grieving for John, but I have started to go back to church..., and I'm playing bridge with my old group again..., and I've joined a bowling league. Does that make you happy?" A small smile played around the corners of her mouth.

I said, "Yes it certainly does. I know you loved John, and you will likely always grieve for him, but you will just get better able to cope with it as time goes on. You were also depressed, and that was making the coping part go very badly. The testosterone has plugged into those receptor sites in your brain cells and helped you overcome the chemical cause of depression that was holding you prisoner in that place. **That** is what I really wanted for you." I had learned something valuable, and she had taught me.

The dose of Halotestin must be just enough and **<u>not</u>** too much. I would like to share an amusing visit with one of my early patients. After starting her on the Halotestin schedule, I saw her back to follow up. She said, "Well, I'm myself again." I asked, "What level are you on?"

She responded, "I'm on Level III, but I want to talk to you about that." I said, "What is there to discuss? You are back to your old sex drive, and that is the correct level for you. Just stay there for the next few years."

She paused for a moment and then pressed on, "Sam and I have always gotten along pretty well, but I was always a 'twice-a-week' woman, and he was a 'once-a-day' man. We could be really compatible if I could take a little more of that stuff and become a once-a-day woman! Can I do that?"

I answered, "No, for two good reasons. First, that would be doing more than your ovaries did, and you would almost certainly have overdose effects such as unwanted hair growth, a deep voice, and some acne. And secondly, even if that weren't a problem, any stimulation of your drive above the normal levels you had when your ovaries were doing it, would be only for a few months before it reverted back to your old levels. Just stay where you are and resume your compromising with Sam." Again, the best dose is just barely enough, and never too much. Try to mimic nature, for you cannot improve on her, when she is doing her job normally.

That concludes the objective inventory we do at "hormone review" appointments. After that is completed, we go into the open discussion of her general observations of changes she has experienced since the last adjustment in her program. This part of the visit has taught me a lot about the wide variability in women and their responses to this therapy. For example, one patient noted that, when she got the right level of hormones in her program, she stopped having heart palpitations! I had seen this a few other times and thought it was due to the possible explanation that their hot flashes had been causing an adrenaline release that caused the palpitations. This patient had no hot flashes before and we started her on a minimal dose because she had a high FSH level. In thirty years, I have heard many symptoms that were relieved by the HRT program which I had not previously thought of as being caused by the lack of hormones.

It is not uncommon for a woman to have no history of migraine headaches until the menopause, when the headaches started with a vengeance. When we reached the correct level for those women, their migraines stopped completely! Obviously, a deficiency of estrogens caused these women to have migraines.

I shall not try to relate all these atypical symptoms that can be associated with hormone deficiency, but they do point up the great variability in women, and the need to make each program fit that one woman. Before you tell a patient that her symptom response is not due to her hormones, give it a lot of thought. It just could be that this patient has something new to teach you, doctor! I have learned much from my patients.

E. When to "cycle" and when to start with continuous hormones?

If a patient comes to me having frequent periods during the past year, though they be irregular or not, I recommend that she start on a cyclic program, i.e., estrogens for three weeks out of each four-week cycle and progestins for varying parts of that twenty-one days. When she stops the hormones for the fourth week, normal withdrawal bleeding (sloughing whatever growth has accumulated in the womb) will occur. The only thing worse than having to have a period is having bleeding that is unpredictable and for which a woman cannot plan. If we try to put such a patient on a continuous program, she will almost always have frequent breakthrough bleeding off and on the first year that is totally unpredictable. If we start her off with a cyclic program she can at least plan when her bleeding will occur, and when the womb lining shows it is not responding much to the hormones by the withdrawal bleeding becoming less and less, we are getting close to the time when she will do well on a continuous program.

Eventually, she will have three cycles in a row when the week off hormones results in having no flow. That is the time to switch over to a continuous program.

If the patient comes to me to start HRT with a history that she has not had any uterine bleeding in the past 9-12 months, she is a good candidate to start on a continuous program, i.e., estrogen and progestin given together every day without cessation and do not try to have any withdrawal time in the scheme. More than 90% of these patients will have no breakthrough episodes the first year, and the other 10% will have three or less breakthrough bleeds the first year.

I tell these patients at the outset what the odds are for breakthrough and stress that if they have a few episodes the first year it is no problem, but is only a mild inconvenience she will have to tolerate if she starts out on a continuous program. The 10% that do breakthrough are prepared and not frightened or worried by these events if they happen. If the breakthrough does occur, it is not heavy and lasts from 3-10 days.

Again, I say that I do this because it works and is effective. Do I spend a lot of time talking to and listening to my patients? I certainly do, and it is time well spent. A woman who has been taught how we do things and why, and who has a program custom-built to fit her and improve her quality of life is much more apt to stay on her HRT. Data from most papers on HRT state that only 25-40% of women stay on their HRT programs more than a year or two. Another way to state that is that 60-75% of HRT programs fail.

In my practice, my failure rate is about 10% or less. I personally believe the difference is the individualization of programs and the patient education that goes into each patient. When we recall that 44% of mature women die of coronary disease and another 15-20% die of the sequelae of fractured legs and spines with osteoporosis, success of HRT programs has the potential to save and prolong the quality years of women's lives by a figure of about 60% of mature women. I believe that the investment of time that goes into my patients is worth every minute.

WHEN DOES THE PROGRAM NEED TO BE UPDATED AND ADJUSTED?

The answer to this question is basically quite simple - anytime that symptoms develop that indicate the program is no longer a custom fit. The human body is not a steel machine that is forever the same. It is a dynamic, evolving and magnificent creation which changes to some degree all its life. I have seen most of my patients do well on their HRT programs for three to seven years without the need for changes or adjustments. Almost all do eventually develop symptoms that say their body is receiving either too much or too little hormone.

The most common scenario is that after 5-7 years, the woman calls me either stating that her body needs a reduction of dosage (she remembers what we taught her about the symptoms of being on too much and can make that diagnosis herself), or she relates the symptoms to me and I make the diagnosis and tell her how to reduce her dosage of estrogen, progestin, or androgen. I have seen women taper their dosage every 5-7 years until at the age of 65-70 their bodies will no longer tolerate any HRT. Most of my HRT patients who have been with me long enough have dropped down to a very low dose and stayed at that dose beyond age 70.

As long as the patient can continue to feel well on some HRT, I advise them to continue regardless of age. The ideal program for the last part of a woman's life is HRT, calcium citrate for 1000-1500 mg. of calcium daily, and a diet rich in fresh, organically grown **raw** fruits and vegetables. The most palatable way to get this last item I have found is a product called Juice Plus and a woman can get it through an NSA distributor for about $40/month.

If the day comes when no HRT can be tolerated without symptoms, I advise starting on products like Fosamax, SERMS (like Evista) or calcitonin along with the other two parts of the program, i.e., calcium and fruits and vegetables. Weight bearing exercise is also needed to combat osteoporosis, along with vitamin D and a small amount of fluoride (which is usually in our water that is fluoridated). If the patient decides to take the Juice Plus product, she need not take any other vitamin supplement. A good, general, post-menopausal program is: Hormones (the program custom fitted to your body), calcium, and Juice Plus, five days per week of morning exercise (start the day with this), self-breast examination once per month, annual mammograms, annual well-woman complete physical exam with Pap test depending on the status of the womb (absent or still present), and leading as active a life as your body will allow.

Ben R. Keller, Jr., M.D.

A WORD ABOUT "NATURAL HORMONES"

While I have not had wide experience with these preparations, the experience I have had is that they are usually far less potent. To reach the amounts that will effectively relieve the hot flashes/flushes and prevent coronary disease and osteoporosis, very high doses are required.

Many of the prescription hormones that are being made available to us now are derived from the wild Yam and soy bean and are just as "natural" as the health food store variety of "natural hormones" we hear about.

Black Kohosh is useful in relieving hot flashes/flushes, but has not been shown to be of any value in protecting the coronary arteries or bones or the tissues of the vagina or bladder or brain.

Basically, I have not seen any well done, reliable studies that support the ability of herbs and other "natural" hormones to protect the tissues that the prescription hormones do. Perhaps good studies that document improved blood levels of lipids and reduced coronary death rates and reduced fracture rates and bone mineral density improvement will be done using the Health Food Store variety of "natural" hormones in the near future, but none are available at the present.

I would remind the reader that HRT is no longer treating hot flashes/flushes, but is using these symptoms to arrive at the best program to protect the many tissues in the menopausal woman and protect her quality of life. The health food store variety of hormones only treat the flashes/flushes.

When I have a rare patient who still wants to use the "Health Food Store" hormones, I ask her to please, let me continue to monitor her Bone Mineral Density, blood pressure, and blood lipids (total cholesterol, HDL, LDL, VLDL, and triglycerides) every few years. That way we can at least know whether these "natural hormones" are really doing everything for her body that they should.

CLOSING REMARKS

I tell my patient to stay on her HRT program so that she can pay all her attention to being the same woman she has always been, and not living according to the numbers (years of age). If she attempts an activity and her body tells her it will no longer tolerate that, stop it and respect her body's wishes. As long as her body can still tolerate any given activity, continue it and do not stop it because she has attained any particular numerical age. Just keep on being yourself and enjoy all of life to the full extent of your body's ability.

While I do not order blood hormone levels to monitor HRT therapy for the reasons I have already given, I do watch my patients' blood tests for cholesterol (total, HDL, LDL, and VLDL), triglycerides (fatty acids), thyroid hormone levels, mammograms, DEXA bone density scans, stool occult blood (screening for colon cancer), and chest x-rays (when they are smokers).

I do not try to dictate or command my patients what they must take or do for their health. I advise them a lot, but, by the definition of that word, I cannot get huffy if they do not take my advice. I do not believe any human has or can morally acquire the right to tell another human being what they must do with their body.

I do absolutely require that I be allowed to perform an Annual Well-Woman Complete Physical Examination to do everything I can do to keep them safe, if they wish to enjoy the benefits of HRT. If a patient does not keep her appointment for these exams annually, she is first warned and given a month to get her Annual Physical Exam done and then no further prescriptions for hormones are given or refills authorized.

I had a dear old friend who also used me for her Gyn Doctor who said, "Oh, Ben, we are such good friends. Surely you are not going to make me have that Annual P.E."

I responded, "Yes we are such very good friends, and that is exactly why I am going to be sure that you have that Annual Physical Exam" I mean that to my core. I will take good care of my patients or I shall not take care of them at all. The only medical care I shall give is the best care of which I am capable and have the knowledge to give.

When the insurance companies, the Managed Care Entities, the Health Maintenance Organizations (H.M.O.s, and they are the worst things that ever happened to people in need of health care), and the Prescription Management Entities with their "formularies" demand that I curtail the quality of the Art of Medicine that I try to give to my patients, I shall ignore all of them and they will strangle me out of the private practice of Medicine. I shall then do what any good dinosaur will do and LUMBAR AWAY TO MY TAR PIT.

You, my dear lady, should not accept poor hormone management even when the doctors try to provide excellence, and these modern entities endeavor to force mediocrity on you and your physicians. Hold onto the quality of your health care, but be prepared to work very hard for it and fight for it. You deserve the best, even if you have to pay a bit more for it. It is about the quality of life - **<u>YOUR LIFE</u>**!

I believe sex is a gift to us from a deeply, unconditionally loving Creator. If it is meant only for reproduction of the human species, why don't human females "go into heat" like other mammals do for a brief period; e.g.,two weeks per year, and neither gender even thinks about sex the other fifty weeks of the year? The Creator gave humans sex also for two people who love each other and want to express that love with their heart, soul, and body as fervently as they can, to do so as a sharing of that gift.

There is nothing in the universe that was created to hurt us, but we can use almost any of these gifts in a manner that may cause harm or pain for ourselves or our fellow travelers.

I believe it is a vicious, stupid, and insipid concept that one person "gives" sex to another. The Creator gives it to both people to share, and neither person can give it to the other. It should not be used to control or attempt to control each other. Doing that spoils and cheapens something incredibly beautiful and precious.

We can share sex with each other whenever we want to, as seldom or often as is comfortable for both partners. That can and should continue to be a healthy part of our relationships throughout our whole life. It shouldn't stop at some arbitrary age, but as our bodies slow down and are able to enjoy sex less frequently, we should accept that and continue to have the gift in our own ways with those physical abilities that we have as our bodies age.

Men have a "menopause" or "climacteric," but we have not studied it as well as we have the woman's menopause. Some day that will happen, and male participation in the sex act will remain better after the onset of that period.

Fortunately, we do know enough about the second part of a woman's life to be able to help her have a comfortable and successful sex life as long as she wishes.

When we have a good sexual session, I believe the Creator smiles on us as a loving parent would who has given the children a wonderful gift and is supremely happy to see us love that gift as the Creator intended. We should enjoy <u>all</u> of the gifts in this life as fully as we can, and medical knowledge is continuing to expand to help us do that. Accept it joyfully and embrace it bravely. Do not be afraid to really live!

"You are a child of God...you have a right to be here."

Ben R. Keller, Jr., M.D.

ABOUT THE AUTHOR

Dr. Ben R. Keller, Jr., M.D. is certified by the American Board of Obstetrics and Gynecology, has taught clinical medicine for the University of Texas Southwestern Medical School at Dallas and the University of Colorado Medical School at Denver. He has practiced solo OB-GYN in Arlington, Texas and Glenwood Springs, Colorado. He is a past Treasurer of the Texas Medical Association (T.M.A.), past Treasurer of the Texas Medical Foundation (T.M.F.), and past

Chairman of the OB-GYN Section of the T.M.A. He was voted "Outstanding Young Man of the Year" in Arlington, Texas in 1970. He has a talent for translating scientific, medical jargon into easy-to-understand, plain English. He listens to his patients!

He has developed and explains a method that is not yet commonly used, of building hormone programs that are each custom fitted to his patients, using hormones that patients feel the best taking and that are <u>safe</u>. His method requires minimal, non-expensive laboratory tests and tries to mimic nature as closely as possible, avoiding the "Change of Life." He listens to his patient and teaches her to "listen to" her body, as they work together to find the HRT program that fits her best.

We think you will find him easy to understand, logical, and fun to read. He gives you a little book with a large dose of the truth.